DRAV
SPACE

To Zoe

May your life be full again

love Dawn Beasley

DAWN BEASLEY

HEALING WORDS

europe books

© 2023 **Europe Books** | London
www.europebooks.co.uk | info@europebooks.co.uk

ISBN 9791220140324
First edition: July 2023

HEALING WORDS

Preface

Born of personal experience this anthology is representative of a heartfelt poetry production by Anglo Asian born author Dawn Beasley.

The poetry collection is the fruit of her tragic and extremely difficult experience as a cancer sufferer who lost her ability to paint because of it.

From the first pages we perceive the necessity to find some interior peace that the author reveals gradually finding comfort in her faith: indeed God is always present in her difficult journey, He is a relief, like she passionately describes in one of first poems, 'Comforts':

Perhaps it is that you are feeling
Desolate and alone
But He is there
Despite your grieving
To comfort, also heal
Over the coming days and weeks
We pray God's strengthening power
His hand to hold
His arms embrace
His peace through every hour

The inexorable passing of time takes turns with moments of joy and moments of tears and pain.

Mercy and grace are sought with the desire to overcome that deep vulnerability that makes her weak, defenceless but nonetheless always hopeful.

Sometimes nightmares materialise, sometimes she finds herself in a tunnel with no end, with events overlapping.

What Dawn demonstrates is that from traumatic events it is possible to recover if we are close to God.

Her poetry reflects a cathartic process of releasing anguish and the building up of hope and faith.

A gathering of thoughts beautifully written, passionately assembled and executed.

Acknowledgments

To my dear husband Roger whom I am indebted to standing alongside me through endless years of heartache, illness, sorrow and grief. Though we faced many trials we have had an incredible journey of faith and ministry to others that has enabled us in all these circumstances. I began to write in the midst of such pain and grief.

I am forever grateful for our two very special adopted daughters without whom much of this book would not have been written.

My work is the unfolding of events I both witnessed and experienced over the years. I found that writing released tension amidst suffering and that words would flow freely as I did so. Many friends including authors Nick and Lois Cuthbert and also the late Craig Dinsell encouraged me to publish my writings most of which are quite short but they can sum up in a few sentences or a poem exactly what that person needs to hear.

Introduction

HEALING WORDS

There is not a circumstance or event in our lives that I believe God is unaware of. We are different in personality and mindset. Some of us have aspired to great heights while others are still on a journey of discovery. Whatever our backgrounds, abilities or disabilities and whether we use or even can develop our potential are all factors known to God.

'Whether you're angry or whether you're spent, either in grief or continued lament, you need words to release such emotions. I can help. I can supply that in words'.

Personal childhood grief, illnesses that could have silenced hope, dealing with damaged children and young adults, prayer counselling and voluntary prison work led me to seek God's heart. What would He say to the hurting? I found a freedom in writing and in speaking because I took the time to listen to God throughout. I found that what I put in words had and still has the effect of releasing people in distress giving a unique and potent perspective for each individual.

It may even be humour that people need! I have been writing for twenty years but have only now decided to publish my work.

I am very grateful to still be alive. It would appear that there is more for me yet to do and share even with my near death illness in 2004 and later an aggressive cancer journey in 2013 both involving surgery and endless months of recovery.

My heart's desire is to enable individuals to see that the pursuit of and trust in God is not a futile journey but one of profound faith that can equip in every circumstance.

Dawn Beasley

CAN YOU LIFT THE PIANO?

They know I can't do that, so why do they say it? It gets me really mad. I'm very cross because I want to know, and they won't tell me. All they keep saying is, 'Well, can you lift the piano?' It's so stupid them asking.

I want to know. I must know. I think they are hiding something really important from me and I'm getting worried. What if? What if something really bad has happened like in that film I watched at Nanny's? The parents told the little girl they were coming back, and I believed them. And then, that awful thing happened. I can hardly speak. They died in a fire. They are NEVER coming back.

What if that is what they won't tell me? Oh no! That couldn't be, could it? That's what I have to ask them. I have to know that nothing terrible has happened to my Mum.

Ever since I can remember, I've told everyone I've got two mummies and daddies. I can't understand why no-one believes me or is interested when I say so. Why do they act in such a horrid way to me at school? *I call the people I live with 'mummy' and 'daddy', but they're not really.* I'm going to be with my own Mum soon.

"If you really want to talk about it, you'll have to wait until Daddy comes home," Mummy said gently.

I leapt out of my chair and into the hall as soon as I heard daddy's car on the drive. "No, sit down!" Mummy said firmly, "and let Daddy have his tea first."

I waited patiently. He seemed to take an age to finish. I couldn't wait anymore, "nothing like that ever happened to my real Mummy, did it?"

There was such a long pause. I felt scared inside. Daddy took me in his arms and sat me on his lap, and Mummy was very still. I tried not to look at her because I was frightened, and sometimes she seemed so serious. "Darling, I have to tell you that your Mummy is dead," he said quietly. He spoke tenderly to me for ages, but I couldn't hear another word after that. I felt dead inside. A knife had struck my heart and I was weeping, crying frantically. It couldn't be. I felt I was drowning. Not one ounce of hope left. I was never going to meet her.

But I had spent my life dreaming of the day when I would, what I would say to her, what she might look like. It was a horrid dream. "Please, stop it and let me wake up!" - "But I never got the chance to say goodbye to her!" And by now the tears were pouring down my face. They were so kind to me. They had such love in their eyes, but it was no good. It wasn't going to bring my own Mummy back.

It was then they showed me a picture from a book, and read something to me from it. Then the book disappeared, for a very long time, and although I asked about it, they wouldn't tell me where it was. I decided in my mind that I would find it again one day. They said that when I was stronger and older, I could have "the information." I am beginning to hate them. How dare they keep me from my real Mummy!

GRIEF DENIED

Did you know of the tears we cried?
When your mother died
Yes, when your mother died?
It was all so confusing
For her death
It seemed intrusive even then
And we wept so many tears
On your behalf
Throughout the years
Through all those years
Tell me, what were we supposed to do?
For now we had adopted you?
You had come to join our family
And you completed our identity
And we loved you
Oh, how we loved you!
And we still do
The journey's been an uphill climb
We'd thought that it would be just fine
But it hasn't been, no, it hasn't been
But we're still praying
Now that's the point I want to make to you
That your Maker knows what's best for you
He's got a plan that's best it's true
So try believing
Yes, try believing

DESERT SPRING

I am in a dry and barren land
The wilderness is more familiar
Than I would like
I am parched and weary
Is there no future?
No solace for my grief?
Surely there is hope
In You Lord God

EMOTION PROTECTION

I've become locked into the rut of my emotions
Locked out by those words - Exclusion zone
I feel angry and hurt and desperately sad
Why should I react so strongly or suffer so acutely?
Is it because I am yet unhealed?
I think You need to touch that core of rejection Lord
I know when it was ... You know too
Will it ever be healed?
Can You make me whole?
Psychological scars take for ages to fade
Especially when inflicted at so early an age
And by those we could never imagine would
betray us
Come and touch my pain Lord
It is so very deep - I lay it bare before You now
Not to cover it again
Except with Your love and healing balm
I'm trusting You for the way ahead
For the future that You say belongs to me
Help me walk in my inheritance

PAIN RELIEF

Lord, take off every layer
Each layer that causes pain
The pain that comes from grief
That costs us unbelief
And wrap me round with love
Your love that does abound
And put Your joy within
For there I will be found

"The children are so resilient!" she said in full flow, and completely ignoring wide eyed Gemma with her mother, who sat opposite Susan Ellis, the Consultant Psychologist. It was only her second visit, and Gemma bit her lip nervously.

Ms Ellis talked quickly and quietly, while Gemma wondered when she would pause for breath. She was watching her broad chin which seemed to gather momentum as her lips spouted a profusion of words she hardly heard. Gemma could never concentrate on long sentences.

She was already visiting her 'other world' which was far safer than sitting in Child Psychiatry. Why couldn't they leave her alone anyway?

She didn't want to talk about 'secrets' because it made her feel really uncomfortable. Her skin tightened around her clenched fists and she rubbed one thumb over the other for comfort. How could she escape?

It was what her mum called, "an ordeal."

FROM ME TO YOU

I'm grateful
Successful or not, I have survived.
I made it through rejection, separation and isolation.
I had few friends at school
Was bullied at home
I experienced depression for years
But I found God, or rather He found me.
Sometimes it feels lonely
When you cannot voice your pain
And silence shrouds your heartache time and time again
Clouds of desperation so easily envelop
But then we must remember, hope is not far away
We are not alone because the Creator is near,
so very near.

HE COUNTS MY TEARS

The obstacles along my path
Are thorny, spiked and long
And I know I have not planted
In my garden this sad song
So I turn to You again, dear Lord
And plead with You for grace.
For no-one else can really know
The trials that I face
When hope is dim, I still cry out
Because You know my heart
And even though I'm weary
It's the place where You impart
That peace and restoration
That inner strength, Your touch
For weak and burdened travellers
The ones You love so much

WHO IS THE PATIENT?

For a duration of thirty, maybe forty minutes
The tension mounted first distanced in silence
Then the odd comment between him and his daughter
Time ticking on impatience rising
Two more daughters descended from
'the room upstairs'
Where children disappear for a while…
Why the tirade of abuse and foul language
In the presence of one so small as she?
And he paced and paced back and forth
The air explosive with rage
The swearing continuous
Looking for an audience
And applause
Difficult to look elsewhere
And keep collection of one's thoughts
To retain personal pain
In such an atmosphere
While waiting with my daughter
What hope for them?
What help for us?
I thought there
Seated in that chair

DEVASTATION

Why did I battle so hard, Father God
And labour so long
For my child?
I asked Your protection
Your strength
And Your shield
I fasted
And prayed
Your sword I did wield
Was it all futile
No value at all?
My strong intercessions,
My heartfelt toil?
I reached out to You God
Put trust in Your Word
It seems almost to me Lord
That You have not heard

Successful or not
I have survived
I made it
Through rejection
Separation, isolation
Was bullied at home
I experienced depression for years...
But I found God
Or rather He found me

Sometimes it feels lonely
When you cannot voice your pain
Your silence shrouds your heartache
And clouds of desperation envelop
It is then you have to remember
Hope is not far away
You are not alone
And the Creator is near
Very near
Build my character Lord

HELP ME BEAR GOOD FRUIT

Lord, help me not to judge
Or criticise
So that I may be able
To see clearly
I'm asking You
For all my needs
Our needs
This day Father
Practical, physical and spiritual
Help me be wise
I want to continue
To walk the narrow road
With You Lord
The road that leads to Life
Help me bear good fruit
Fruit that is recognisable
As produce of a life empowered
Based on my Saviour
The Rock Who is Christ Jesus
For He is my firm foundation

COMFORTS

Only God can give you comfort
Solace for your pain
May He hold
Give strength
Empower you
Every day sustain
For now it seems
That hope is waning
Despair it overwhelms
Fear invades
Each conscious thought
Yet God pours out His peace

Perhaps it is that you are feeling
Desolate and alone
But He is there
Despite your grieving
To comfort, also heal
Over the coming days and weeks
We pray God's strengthening power
His hand to hold
His arms embrace
His peace through every hour

FROM BATTLE TO SANCTUARY

The impasse of confrontation, again
Any notion of guidance and of framework
Unlocks those torrents of abuse
Denial and accusation
Where there can be no resolution
Nor healing for that moment in time
And we retreat
Battle scarred and weary
To that only safe place
The arms of God
And into the Sanctuary once more
Where comfort and peace are present

CRITICAL THOUGHT

I mustn't
Criticise
Or shout
Unwise replies
She shouldn't
Vent her spleen
Upon us both
For shattered dreams

MARKS FOR ACHIEVEMENT

A solitary figure
Stunningly beautiful
And small in height
She seemed so out of place
Amongst the other teenagers there
Only one year left for taking their qualifications
How any of those kids
Achieve anything academic at all
Is a wonder
What is normal schooling
Amongst these poorly youths
Normality for them
Is scoring one's skin
Not marks for achievement
No revision here late into the night

BURIED TREASURE

Lord, my heart is aching
I'm wrestling with a pain
So deep within
It's a mother's heart
I know full well.
But it prevents not the flow of grief
And never will
For unfulfilled hope
Nurtures disappointment
Well, not so much hope really
As watching
Treasure buried, sullied
Separated from mind and body
And distanced, as if it never were
And tarnished there
For lack of use
I pray hope will surface
Before it is too late
To resurrect
To yield a hundredfold
Bring life from death
Reveal Your strong and mighty power
Yes, Lord release Your peace

WILD CHILD CARE

You say you would send her back
Would you? Could you?
I know your care for her is intense
For your 'wild child'
And it would break your very heart if she left
Or, God forbid, 'departed' this world

All the insults hurled, would be lost
In the waters of endless despair
And unfulfilled hopes
And you would be empty
Just like she is now

Let Me have your raging
Tempestuous storms of emotion
Drink in great gulps of My grace
With yet more of My love
Trust me now

For this is when your independence hinders
And obstructs again like hers
Pin your anger and grief to Me
Let go and if you will allow
I will help you again

SORROWFUL SONG

It's far from easy, You know that Lord
You never said it would be a piece of cake
But You never told us how painful
Just how very painful our lives would be
Or how many years we should have to endure
Of strife, of testing and rejection
How hard it is to watch the withdrawal of your child
Not the natural breaking loose for adulthood
But the unnatural defiance and full blown rebellion
That we have lived with now for so long
Its' consequences have reaped a sorrowful song
Inside our hearts and we are weeping still

GOLDEN INCENSE BOWLS

I seem to have wept an ocean of tears
Over the years, and I was thinking, Lord
Surely, its time for weeping to cease?

Lord, I want to ask please
Has my suffering yet produced
Some beautiful fragrance?
Or is there more intensity of pain
To be pressed out still?

Are the golden incense bowls
Filling with my intercessions?
Are they nearly filled, Lord?

You alone know the limits of endurance unto death
No-one has been stretched beyond Your Cross
Therefore, no-one but You can comprehend
The depths and toll of my grief and loss
Receive my burden then at the altar of sacrifice

NO REJECTION

When she told me that
My dreams, they died
I died inside
Tried to hide my pain
And ceased to be
I denied my hurt
Decided to leave
As soon as I could
It wasn't my home
I didn't belong

The pain, it surfaces
Time and again
It's hard to suppress
Takes all my energy
Sometimes I manage.

I disconnected from reality
Distanced myself from them
Grew cold and hard
Would not associate
And certainly not respect

WHO do they think they are?
Telling me what to do
I'll not listen
If I become a 'bad' girl
Perhaps they'll reject me

It's not working at all
My plans always fail

My anger is rising
Aggression comes swift
But they remain

I hurl abuse
Lie and blaspheme
Run rampant
Out of control,
And still they are there

I cannot submit,
I've gone too far
Become hateful
In every respect
I can't turn back

I'm out to blame them.
They deserve punishing
For all my hurt
Despite all their love
I'm in self destruct mode

It's all consuming
This hatred inside
And it's distorting me
Will you help me God?
I can't breathe or live if you don't

REMINISCENT

I watched, somewhat at a distance
You seemed, almost 'reminiscent'
If only I could re-awaken
Memories you've now forsaken
Now you've removed my only key
You've locked me out. Why can't you see?
Lord, please will you open the eyes of her heart
For her to know peace with the joy You impart

LIKE ACID TO THE SKIN

It's like a living bereavement this daily path I walk
For my child that is lost and yet she still lives
Every day the grief rises and often overwhelms
For years I fought her battles
Defended her cause, came to her rescue
It took me so very long to wake
To see, to contemplate her loss
The depth of our suffering
I was fearful
And bewildered by her actions and reactions
Her cutting prematurely loose
Her self- harming and addictive behaviours
Her emerging anger and rage fired relentlessly
Toward any who dared to ask a question
That touched her pain
Watching a loved one spiral down
Into the pits of despair
Of sin and of hopelessness
Without the realisation of reality
And recognition of truth
Is like acid to the skin
We live in a dry parched desert
Constantly waiting for the rains to come
Watching for the rainbow
Awaiting our prodigal's return

VICTIM SUPPORT

When do your feelings cease to find expression?
Is it possible the gaping emptiness
Can be filled and trust renewed?
Can restoration be?
And prophecy fulfilled?
I hope this will come to pass
This side of eternity
For the waiting does seem eternally long

Our hearts never cease to ache for her
Despite the years we have suffered
It is very strange to explain this struggle
From a parents' perspective
And yet, we are the victims of an assault
From the one we hold so dear
Currently she will not own us as her parents
She exists inside a whirlwind of hate

CARE FOR WOUNDED SOULS

Tears are seeping out my being
I can't contain the pain
Our work as parents is complete
We have 'passed with honours'
But she dismissed our covering as refuse
The responsibility we held as 'dung'
Disowned, rather that submission sung
Impossible task
To parent a rebel
Have to view it differently
The honour - to care for a wounded soul
To love unconditionally

OUR INTERCESSIONS

Lord, please destroy the 'rod of pride'
Turn falsehood and lying to that of truth
Stop the mockery that understanding will come
Remove fools from her path that only signpost
a path of death
So that instead, she will seek goodness and prudence
In order to consider her steps
Guard her haste and short temperedness
Help her plan good and not plot evil
Please grant her unfailing love and faithfulness
Help her work hard, witness truthfully, fear You Lord
For 'Fear of the Lord is a life giving fountain'
That offers escape from the snares of death
Help her follow Life, control her anger,
have the right attitude
A heart for the poor, and seek a refuge with You Lord
That she might relinquish sin and gain wisdom
And therefore an understanding heart O Lord

KEEPING FOCUS

Over the years
I've faced many fears
And suffering long
Have continued on
To trust You Lord
Despite great pain
Enduring grief
Time and again
Nothing is resolved
With time or words
They cannot fill
The empty hole
Or stick plaster
On the wound
Nor hope to heal
Only Jesus can do that
So that's what I'll continue to do
I'll keep looking to Him
To see me through
For He's reliable
Always there
Trustworthy, pure
Completely true

Are there denominations in heaven?
Then for which one did Christ die?
Didn't Jesus come to save mankind?
The proud and hateful
Independent lost?
Not those whose clubs dictate
Rules, their membership states
No, clearly, this was not the Father's plan
Rather, provision of relationship
Between God and man
A love response
To touch the heart
And cleanse the wounds of sin
It's dark and stubborn stain
Washed in Christ's blood
Makes white as snow
Restores us one with God
Gives Life
Gives Hope again!

SALVATION RAP

You're back
I'm back....YEAH
Where have you been?
What have you seen?
Oh that?
Yes, that!

WELL ..
You know that bit of history
That bit that's quite a mystery?
Yeah, well I brought it to the Cross man
Boss man for lost man
And it's gone!
It's gone! How come?
Did you lose it?
Yeah, I lost it
Well, not really, but it's gone!
Oh really?
Yeah really!

And I got a great replacement
In the Person of God's Son
God's Son?
God's Son! He's the One
If we let Him
You let Him?
Yeah, I let Him
He deals with our behaviour stuff
Gets to the core and that's enough
For our healing
Your Healing? Yeah, healing

And of course, a closer walk
So it's not just talk
It's of value
Yeah, value
Real value!

RAZOR SHARP

She erased my character
With a cruel slice of words
They pierced deep into my spirit
My mind and my soul
Her sentence
Razor sharp
Her understanding dull
What point any challenge
When hearing is but dim
And sight is blinded
Integrity wiped out?

UNTIMELY DEATH

Untimely death sounds
No coherent preparatory note
Its sudden arrival
Unsung symphonies
Come swift
In culminating chorus
Of words unsaid
Perhaps regret
Our memories remain
And God sustains
He does, He heals
If we permit Him
To enter our hidden world
Of pain and grief
There is no easy way
To walk this path
This journey of life
While we continue along
With heads bowed
But if we will lift our glance
And trust in God
And Jesus His own Saviour Son
We would ultimately
See such a world
Around us
Of creative beauty
That would literally astound
With the power and presence
Of God's love

DROWNING

Help me! Help me please someone!
I feel like I'm sinking
The water is up to my ears
I can't catch my breath
Quick! I'm going under
Come now to rescue me

It's like when I'm in bed at night
Under the bedclothes
Where no-one can see
I feel safer there
And I am alone, just me
But the darkness isn't my friend anymore
As I'm feeling so frightened now

I wanted you to notice me
But my game it has all gone wrong
It's just because of those words
That you said 'Not now, maybe later' again
But I wanted to tell them I'm not good like you are
As I thought they'd let me join in
It all went wrong
They hate me, I know
I feel like running away
Everyone's cross
They're talking behind my back
Whispering plans
That I can't understand

PLEASE, don't make me go there
I just want to be with you

That's all I need
But you don't understand

IS THIS MY CHILD?

I am not sure that I recognise her
Or even want to at this time
Though I know she is in need
She will not let anyone help her

It is difficult
As some will know

Shouting, screaming
Ranting, raving
Shrieking, banging
Stomping, stamping
Swearing, slamming
Thieving, fighting

We will still pray on
Despite every obstacle

REVERSE ACCUSATION

We have endured long term abuse
And yet it seems we are accused
The charge that we are 'lacking love'
'We have not cared, nor guidance shown'
What mockery is this our Father?
For You alone have seen our plight
And travelled with us through this night
Of endless tears and years of pain
We turn to You time and again
Hear this, our plea, O God once more
Revive, redeem our daughter, Lord

BEREAVEMENT

We are grieving
The loss of our child
She is not dead
My heart it bleeds so
You know
I cannot bear this pain
No more inside of me
This separating
From my daughter's love
You see, it hurts me
And it kills me dead

Let me hold you forever
And tell you I never
Stopped loving you
Daughter of mine
I know I got cross
For all of the loss
It destroyed so much of my hope
So I shed many tears
Through all of those years
For your childhood it went
Education was spent
And that was my cry
My honest and heartfelt lament

GARMENTS OF PRAISE

There is no measure on 'Suffering' my friend
That is more costly or less painful
Than another's trial

Your Journey has been equally long
You have endured indescribable pain
It is not less than ours
Nor ours more intense than yours

Your wardrobe is more varied than that
The clothes hanging there are costly indeed
You only fear to wear them

I see they are the Master's robes
And what He has produced in you
Throughout the years has endless worth
Perhaps you bear some hidden pain
Its wounds unhealed, unyielded
Which prevent your 'putting on'
This Mantle of Praise
The Lord Himself has given you

There is no separation from His Love
Remember that
For He would lift your chin
And smile and say that you
Yes you are Precious in His sight!

That is the word that far outweighs
All earthly value here
And must be worn

For jewels such as yours
Are to be seen
And not hidden away

THE DESERT OF ISOLATION

I experienced the pain of exclusion once more
Not so much a specific act
But the fact of not being included
Or thought about, only abused
Cut very deep
Upon the already painful scab of rejection
It brought me to the Desert of Isolation
Where complete and utter loneliness
Shrouds a dying heart
Were it not for the message of hope in Christ
I would long have ceased to exist
But here I am
Reminded that my real destiny
Is one with a future
And one with my heavenly Father
When I arrive at this realisation
I am able to fling off the dirty rags
Of oppression, and clothe myself
With the garments of salvation
I put them on and I stand and gaze
At the splendour and glory of my God
Praise His Name!

SPEECH THERAPY

No-one who is unacquainted with self criticism
Should be allowed to blacken another.
Sullying their character by negative
and damaging comments
It is a constant injustice we view without objection
Much like the bystander watching an innocent victim
Being physically assaulted as if glued to a TV screen
Rather than interfere and make a scene
To divert the protagonist's attack
And neither should we contain our silence as if mute
For if bitter arrows are fired and shot
They inflict great damage on their victims
intentional or not
One slice of the outrageous tongue let loose
Cuts quick and deep on unsuspecting ears and hearts
And such profanity must cease if the culprit
Of this slanderous flow continues in destructive mode
They will themselves fall victim to their own tongue
And such will be the consequence
They will negate friendships and loyalty will also wane
Not until they awaken to their own need
And realise the help and healing God provides
To touch humanity at source and take on board
His call to all
To esteem the other greater than themselves
Will they themselves be restored and made whole

CRY OF DESPERATION

Father, come and help us
We've cried out to You for such a long time!
We've seen glimpses of hope
Traces of daylight between darkness
Between storms
But where are You Lord in this desert
This abyss, this dark valley, this weary night?

I don't know how to pray another prayer
All my intercessions are lodged with You
You know my every sigh
You see each teardrop fall
You feel my pain
And all my fears too

What's happening Lord?
I don't see any wind of change yet
Surely a door will open soon
Can You just reassure us she's safe with You
And that You'll see her through this, please Lord

THE RIGHT VENUE FOR REHAB

Lord, we cry out for Your specific help and intervention
We have reached a blocked road with no possible access
We don't have to make any more choices
You have decided for us that it is enough
We have done all and it is over
Breakthrough, O God, is what we pray!
Bring us release, we can't wait anymore
We can't do or effect anything further for her
The time for parting has arrived
Let it be in Your place of healing
Of restoration and of hope O God
You have promised to provide all of our needs
And we need respite. We cry out for Your mercy
Provide a place of safety and of challenge
And of facing up to her own issues please
You open the door
Everyone has reached the end of knowledge
And of human possibilities
Do something now that is right for her
As well as a God opportunity we pray
We can't think where it should be
Or where that should come from but You know
Bring an end to this torment for each of us

A PARENT'S HEARTFELT CRY

Today she is departing on a journey long
It's a time that seems to have been forever coming
But now she has to suddenly face her issues
She is with child
And she needs to learn rapidly all about motherhood
But first she must address
The pains of her own childhood
Something until now she has fought against
She is at the end of a road
And the beginning of another
We pray she will walk this one with You,
Sovereign Lord

DEPARTURE

What can we say to you this day?
What could we pray we haven't yet prayed?
We love you
Have not ceased in our caring
Despite all the struggles
Despite years of pain
We bless you as always
Again and again
Dearest daughter
You are the child that the Lord gave
May He take you and form you
And heal all your hurt
Bless and reveal to you
Plans he has just for you
And bring you safe
On the path that you travel
Protecting you and your child
In the years that unravel

JOY IS MISSING

JOY Lord....is missing
We are so battered and bruised
And though we have the keys
I think the lock has been changed
How can we lift our praises
When the means by which we praise
And that which has brought You glory
Has been removed?
Was it robbed with Your approval?
Is it an oversight
That You haven't replaced this outlet yet?
Are You going to give it back?
Are there any conditions, any terms
Which need to be settled in advance of receipt?
Won't You tell us *please Lord!*
Or has Your letter got lost in the post?
Please could You break silence over this
And let us have a clear answer!

TEARS AGAIN

So weepy today
Isolation envelops the mind
Catches the heart off balance
Deflects sanity
Security lies in one truth
God is
He is ever present
Loving, caring, giving
The Rock on which we stand
Therefore, despite the storm
Or battle raging
We hold fast to God, our Saviour
Who alone can quiet the winds
Make battles cease
Reinstate our sanity
Yes, whether He chooses
To release or relieve us of such pain
Is His choice alone
Mine is to trust Him further

RELINQUISHMENT AND GRIEF

We are right beside you
And we raise you up in prayer
For our God Who rules the heavens
Is before you everywhere

We had to let you go my love
As we'd been told to do
It was the hardest of decisions made
Trusting God to see you through

SPIRITUAL DISABILITY

You see, the Lord looks on the heart
He doesn't say, "How excellent is your intellect!"
But rather, I would have you obey me, my child
In intimate response to Me
Not words on words
Expressed or silent thought
For, as much as you think your mind expands
When your spirit is closed, it shows
And you disabled are

What do you think that encounter with God
should produce
If faith in only shallow soil remains?
Then roots will not grow deep
Nor will the person mature
For when the heart is touched by God Himself
Their very being comes alive and testifies
And you have seen this witness friend
So will you also now respond?

WEEDS IN MY GARDEN

When I looked at my sadness and grief, I noticed that the weeds in my garden were taking root and plants of sin namely anger, hurt and rejection were springing up all around and were crushing peace and hope within me.

All I could see was marred with negative thinking, criticisms of what people had or hadn't done in my eyes because I was feeling so wounded.
Jesus understands all this and yet He is free to love and to forgive and He shows compassion on everyone.
I exchange all the hurt and being wronged instead for His joy and love as the way I now choose to live.

THE KING'S CLOTHES

My dearest love
Have you seen the clothes
The King has bought?
They're all for you
For you to wear
You need to choose
To put them on
For they've been purchased
Just for you!
There's every type
Of garment there
Which when put on
Display a beauty
And a radiance too
Even armour is supplied
For battles you
Will need to fight
It's time for you
To rise up now!
Put on the clothes
The Saviour purchased
With His blood
It cost His death to bring you life.

SHEPERD TO LAMB

Allow yourself some sleep this day
And when you wake, sit quiet
Rest now my lamb
Receive My strength
Inhale My breath of life within
Let healing rivers flow
For I have seen your needs dear one
The weariness within
Take time yourself to be restored
To know My touch
And hear My Spirit's voice

THE SIGNIFICANCE OF FAILING

The point isn't my failing
Rather it is God's sense
Of making me into the person
He intends for me to be
God is working out His salvation
At the place of my brokenness
What do You intend for me then Lord God?
How will I most fulfil Your plan in my life?
Oh, I see, I need to praise You
So that what I have thought
Was failure and weakness
Can actually lead
To Your strength and wholeness!

SOLACE IN GRIEF

When you have known a loved one long
And when they've sung a happy song
Their loss would seem to overwhelm
As grief and pain invade our thoughts

Yet at this time God's comfort comes
He sends His Spirit to our side
We find our peace in Christ alone
And greater solace than we've known

PIERCED ARE THE HANDS OF LOVE

I have a gift of love for you
You will find many precious thoughts
Each individually wrapped
I hope you like each item there
I gave my heart inside each one
As time goes by, my heart it grieves
Unfolds the hurt contained within
Of deep regret and pain
And then my thoughts run wild once more
And feelings of rejection merge
With anger and distress
What must I do to earn your love?
I try to speak, it comes out wrong
And my insistence overwhelms
All hope of happy song
I've got to learn, I know, I try
But you have shut the door so tight
I guess the LORD must feel this way
With gifts that He has given us
We say we have received them all
But they remain unwrapped each one
His Love, His Grace, His Peace, His Joy
How painful is the Saviour's cry!

HEALING FOR BROKEN VESSELS

And still, behind closed walls I sit,
make comment on the world,
While silent tears drip down my face,
and I a prisoner am
I feel betrayed by all my friends,
and those ones closest by
Have even voiced complaint to me,
which raise my heartfelt cry
For here, I am so widely used, in ministering grace
I hear and see their needs so dear.
Release their pain, give hope again.
But, can I always see this fruit?
And can I ever 'wisely' speak? I sadly answer, "No."
I need God's help myself, in restraining of my speech
For kindly thoughts, for gracious words.
The work is not completed yet
Echoes of my childhood days when I expected praise,
Are silenced by "not good enough!"
Or "you have failed!"
I need to clearly change my ways
But how, I wonder tell me please?
For words, they trip right off my tongue
I need God's help
I need His power
Please Saviour, will you come!

THERE IS MORE

When you don't know what to say,
How to pray,
You should know,
It's God Who hears
When your heart is filled with sadness
No more gladness
Tears are present
So are fears
When you think that strength has gone
You cannot sing another song
It's okay, no need to worry, say you're sorry
God will hold you in His arms
He'll pour out His healing balm
He will strengthen and sustain
Enfold you, time and time again
He understands the grief you bear
He WILL surround you with His care
God will help you and He'll guide
Give you wisdom stand beside
Allow Him now to heal, give strength
For your life, throughout its length
Only trust and simply tarry
Let Him all your burdens carry

CRACKS IN MY MIRROR

What is the mirror I hide behind for self preservation and protection, and why? Things that mark my insecurity or basic lack of confidence are all the more quickly revealed these days!

It only takes a sentence, or a few words, to pull down any apparent image of self confidence! You would think my internal plumbing supply was faulty or in need of a service! The valves obviously need to be tightened to prevent all such leaks or do they?

After all, I only had honest words with the Father this morning
asking Him to change my heart, and to apply those aspects that are yet unrefined as I really need His transformation.

If I want to be like Him and reflect His love, this is vital. Yet the instant a comment was uttered that threatened, or more accurately that which I 'felt' threatened, those previously dry cheeks became quickly moistened!

"Don't give up on me, Father!
I meant what I said.
Please apply Your lessons to my heart!"

When you have endured a lengthy trial
A sustained battle
And have stayed the course
And succeeded
It is important
Actually vital
That you allow for rest
And restoration
As a priority
Do not hurry in this
You have been in the front line
Now let God minister to you
Let Him enfold you in His love
Wrap you round with His comfort
And give you daily even hourly strength
But take your time
To rest in Him
Let God's Spirit fill you up

DI .... STRESS

What was it you was supposed to do
To find out.. 'what was really true?'
We all have faults, yeah, so do you
You aint listened to the story all ways thru.

You heard one side .. you never asked the other,
And you was angry at him who'd been like a brother.
But what if they haven't really done
All those things she says, then what, son?

What if her perception was a judgement instead
Of what she 'thought' she saw that was just in her head?
She could have stormed off raging home to you
And if you stop and think, yeah that could be true.

You know what? You haven't checked it out.
Don't you think they know when you're stressed,
you shout?
It's time don't you think that you heard their side?
Do they normally lie, do they normally hide?

You reactin' this way, it aint helping you
They've shown in the past that their love is true.
They're for you not against,
you must know that by now.
Get rid of this gripe, you got to sort it somehow.

I know in their hearts, they mean you no harm,
And I guess all this stuff has caused great alarm.
That's the devil's way, to divide and to spoil,
But let God pour out His healing oil.

IRRELEVANT

My advice is not heeded
It's just not received
And I am not included

I feel so rejected
They care nothing at all
They are quite unaware

I thought they would know
From my silence
That I completely withdrew

Those tears that I shed
Revealed innermost pain
So deep inside my heart

So Lord I would ask
As I draw aside
For healing once again

THERE IS HOPE

Only God can heal
Only He reveal
The damage that's behind the mask
We try to wear
It is only God Who sees
And He who understands
The hurt, the pain, the cost
Of what has been undone
For He the Healer is
The One who binds our wounds
The One who tells us truth
The One who makes us whole

THE BREAD PRAYER

Feed me Jesus so I may be fed and nourished
Feed me so I may be able to function
Feed me so I may be full of You
Of Your Word, Your direction
But let me listen
Let me take in all You are saying to me
And only let me move in obedience
To Your direct Word when You give it
And only go when You tell me to
LORD, if I don't dwell in Your lovely Presence
If I don't receive all You have to give me
I will have nothing to share
But let me so meditate on Your Word
My daily 'Manna'
And then I will know when to move
Or when to be still and wait

WELL DONE, HERE'S YOUR CROWN

Do not feel regret my friend
The scales are not for you to weigh.
Whoever dreamt you walked not straight?
Or failed to love, or give or bless?
You thanked the Lord for each new day
Gave praise and worship to the King!
You spent your life in serving Him.
You've grown in wisdom, power and grace.
You're greatly loved, so please fear not.
Don't judge yourself o'er 'who' you are.
Leave that to God, and try to rest!
Let His embrace enfold you now.
Receive His love, His care for you
And never fear what man may say
It's GOD to Whom you're answerable!
And this I know, He'll say to you
"Well done, that servant, here's your crown!"

INCONSISTENT PROPENSITY

Inconsistency has the propensity
To cause instability
Even disability
Of mind and intellect
That can lead to a disconnect
And therefore a profound effect
Upon the brain and personality
Losing time and functionality
When a change of direction
Would aid this correction
To align the gut and brain
To activate again
The neural pathways thus to fire
So that the person can aspire
To all that God intends
In their being to commend

RE-ALIGNMENT

What do we do when we're not believed?
When what's been said has carried such grief?
The damage, it scars, when people accuse
Friendship is broken as well as our trust
When they don't know the truth
The hurt it runs deep
A sadness such that it makes us weep

And is there a way to go forward from here?
I think there is, but it's not too clear
Yes, the guilty ones must indeed repent
And we're to forgive, in Christ's own strength
But can we trust again? I'm not really sure
Discernment's required, with Love that's pure

The way ahead is to follow Christ
To read God's Word, and hear from Him
So that when He speaks, we'll act and do
Whatever He says, He'll guide us through
We don't know the answers ahead of time
But we'll trust He'll advise, direct, re-align

WHEN FAITH IS TRIED

You are brave beyond measure
You're My child, You're My treasure
You know, I am with you
For I stand beside
I know you walk with Me
Though faith it is tried
I'll never forsake you
In death or in life
Allow Me your burdens
And all of your strife
Now, let Me embrace you
Hold fast in My love
Grace all sufficient
And Peace from above
Take hold of My Word
With its promises true
They're there to receive now
And they are for you

AUTUMN LEAVES

When you watch a person die
You may cry and wonder "Why?"
You might tremble in your spirit
You might scream and shout and rant
But empty words in empty vessels
Will not heal your aching heart
Only God can touch that pain
It's time to turn to Him again

ENGAGING IN BATTLE

I will trust You Lord
Though severe this pain
I am near despair
I cry out again
We've travelled on
This journey long
Put faith in You
And prayed so strong
And yet our hopes
Are dwindling Lord
We still believe
We draw Your sword
O help us in this battle now
And please pour out Your mighty power

GRACE IS THE SOLUTION

I have quite an amount of faith I believe
It's love that I am lacking in so often
Maybe the connection the Apostle Paul makes
Between a pure heart and a good conscience
Is quite simply the 'key'
Underneath the surface of my skin
Seems a ready trigger
To bite back those who devour me
With a glance or an off- hand remark.
Only grace releases that person
From my wrath
And only grace
Mercy and peace from God releases me
Help me ask for and employ such grace Lord

AT THE MERCY SEAT

Lord, I still carry the marks
Of a wound that is deep
It is also angry and sore,
And I think this is because
Of the damage it did
That could not have hurt me more

You know Lord, I have so many times
Released this person in prayer
I found her words of judgement inflicted
Damaged deep my heart laid bare

I've borne this scar so long unhealed
So I need to let go of this pain
Now I run to You and I humbly cry
"Would You forgive me again?"

That's all that I can voice O God
In obedience to Your Word
For Father, in forgiveness
It is I who'll be set free
I simply release her once and for all
Please give me more grace I pray
I leave the injustice with You, Lord God
And her at Your mercy seat!

GRIEF'S JOURNEY LONG

I took my eyes off from the Lord
And briefly could not view His world
His Word was void, my hope was faint
While hurt and anger raged within
And I the lonely one was lost

As for praise, it ceased in me
To be expressed and voiced out loud
Instead, I drew within myself
And nursed my pain which cut so deep
All hope and peace and joy denied

You know the griefs that I have borne
The unsaid words, the crushing blows
The sadness and the suffering
Physical and emotional Lord
And yet Your Word to me says "Come!"

And come I must or else I die
No other remedy for sin
Though I the injured one remain
I all release, to breathe and live
To be restored to You again

Is it any wonder she silent remains?
Have you yet seen the extent of her pain?
She needs time for healing
Of all she's endured
Of course she has suffered
Watching you in your pain
Expressing your hatred
Time and again
The blows you inflicted
The language, abuse
The refusals, the downslide
Which worsened, and yet
She still kept on praying
Though frightened and sad
Yet she is the one
Who is made to feel bad

It's an incredibly long journey we have travelled on these last few years. It's something we would never want to repeat. Even talking about it causes hidden emotions to rise up and run rampant for a season. It is so very painful. This is because the trauma in its entirety is yet unhealed.

The wound is getting better, don't get me wrong, but there is much internal damage and bruising. We can all appreciate that healing for such depths of pain as we have suffered would of course take a great deal of time to recover from. But if we do not speak and share our vulnerability, you will think all is fine while we travel alone. I have to tell you we are definitely not alone. God has held us close. He has been there for us. He has provided counsel at the deepest moments of our pain with entrusted pastors.

You know, there are many who just do not understand us even now and who avoid us at all costs. They turn their heads so as not to speak to us or cast a critical eye in response to our greeting them and quickly hurry on.

So dear friends, when we hear of your struggles, we are grateful to be able to listen to your own heartfelt pain, to let compassion flow and vulnerability remain.

WHO IS THE VICTIM HERE?

What sparks this fuse that lights the fire?
Why am I made to feel the guilty one?
It is I who has been recipient to your rage
Your torrent of abuse
And witnessed an explosion of your fury
Been sworn and shrieked at
Excluded and ignored
And for why?
Is it because you were challenged?
Or because you had expended so much energy
In trying to achieve what you thought was right
Is anyone questioning that?
This attack is disproportionate my friend
And I do not deserve to be on the receiving end
I am the victim here
And should not be held responsible for your wrath

PRAYER THROUGH TROUBLED TIMES

Father, help us as we pray
Teach us Lord
Just what to say
Lead us through this troubled time
Give us wisdom
Peace of mind
For we place our trust in You
Asking that You see us through

We seem to have travelled a journey of much trial and tribulation for a number of years. Such a journey may appear a lonely road to some and it most certainly is for those of us without faith. Yet when you have the Lord Jesus alongside, the One Who is infinitely acquainted with grief and suffering, you will know that you can access all the resources of heaven to assist in troubled times.

God's grace is always available, at least that is my testimony for I have personally experienced such in my life over numerous issues whether that be physical, mental or emotional. That's why I like to share some of the truths I have learnt along the way to encourage you not to forget to draw on God's strength yourself during difficulty, stress, confusion or desperation.

Life can be like a drawing, its different perspectives unveiling the unique aspects of our walk and our vision, its tones and shades reflecting the depth and detail of reality or even simply an impression caught in a mere glimpse of reality.

I am convinced and really believe that God wants you to know how very valuable you are to Him, that you are not forgotten, and that He is ever present just waiting for you to reach out to Him in times of need. All you have to do is ask Him and He will lead you, help and enable you.

BLURRED VISION

I've felt isolated Lord, these recent months
And if I'm honest the last few years
I've tried very hard indeed
I've applied my mind and worked so hard
At what I thought You gave me to do
But now life is changing, disintegrating
And my vision, which once was quite clear to me
Is blurred and I am left near blind and confused
What's happened, Father?
Can I call You that?
Was I inspired by my self- effort
On a mission without You as Lord?
That never was the intention
You knew that all along
For it's our hearts You read
I'm so glad You understand me
From that perspective
Else I would have given up by now

SIGNPOSTS TO REDIRECT

Were those words
Words of criticism
Aimed to harm?
I ask you to consider
Whether they were
"Signposts to direct you back"
On the straight and narrow road
From whence you came
Words of advice, empty fly
When rebellion strong
Its' onslaught brings
And covers dark
A blanket over godly things

A RUBBER IS NEEDED

Lord, I keep making mistakes
As soon as I open my mouth with certain people
I blunder
Am tactless, thoughtless
And compassion has flown out the window
I don't think
When I should really ask You for help
Also, I fail to really be sensitive
Please forgive me
Please rub out my mistakes Lord
To wash me clean
Above reproach
And live for Your glory
That won't be possible without You
So Lord, will You fill and enable me please
I'd appreciate that

RENEW MY HOPE

Help me please, Lord!
I'm drowning in such sorrow
For my grief, it overwhelms
Though I know, that God, He comforts
I just cannot face this pain
I am trying for my children's sake
To strengthen and direct them
I am sitting down to write
But no words will issue forth
I see the crowd of people
Who are longing to embrace me
I know the strength I have had
Yet I want to run away
Lord, give me space, and help me
For I don't know how to breathe
I know You're by my side, Lord
I know I trust in You
I just cannot feel Your presence
'Til my hope has been renewed

CONSEQUENTIAL JOURNEYS

Yes, it's true that when we listen
We hear their heartfelt cry
And words release
Their pain inside
For them to breathe a sigh
But words contain frustration too
Of brokenness unhealed
And how they view the world
May be partly
What they 'feel'
For if they've lived a life outside
And reaped that which they've sown
It may be their distorted thought
For now is what they own
But what about repentance
For rebellious choice and deeds?
Without it, there's no healing
For every victim's needs
Our records show through heart felt pain
We too have suffered long
And forgiveness is the proof of grace
For this path we've travelled on

SOME OF YOUR OWN MEDICINE

Did they say what you 'think' they said?
Convinced they 'must have' in your head
Were you there, was it clearly heard by you?
Or is it what you 'believe' to be true?
Do you have any proof? What are the facts?
Give me evidence please, not just the axe!
For if you falsely accuse you might do some damage
An' you'll leave that person all alone and ravaged

WEARINESS IN MY SPIRIT

It's been a struggle these last weeks
And is affecting me physically and emotionally
There is a weariness in my spirit which is realised
In a weariness in my body
Lack of energy and strength
Call it what you like
The water leaks unannounced from my eyes
I need space,
Space to be, to think
To pray, to read, to walk
To do nothing, to spend a quiet hour
Without being asked, "what's the matter with you?"
"Go and see a doctor!"
These are demands which are unhelpful
And too intrusive to even reply to
I know they come from love and concern
But I don't have to answer
For my private thoughts
Are kept safe with You, Lord
To be in Your presence
Is my only secure place
Let me tarry there Lord
While I recover

WHERE COMFORT IS FOUND

Find your comfort in God alone
She said, and in my heart
I responded 'yes'
So will I seek You my Father
For all the wasted hours
Of pain could never be
Washed away with tears
Nor could my fears
And though I mouthed the words
Prayers of anguish fuelled unrest
As peace momentarily visited
This house, then flew the nest
And I, disquieted, searched again
For You, and found Your Rock unmoved
And sheltered there
Safe beneath the shadow
Of Your wings

THE PAIN OF LONELINESS

Do we not need the power
And the pain of loneliness
To pry us away from isolation
And push us toward others?
When something bad happens
A painful misunderstanding
With a friend
An ache of guilt
Over some responsibility
That I let slide
I try to view that occurrence
As I would a physical pain
I accept it as a signal
Alerting me to attend
To a matter that needs change
I try to be grateful
Not for the pain itself
But for the opportunity
To respond,
To form good
Out of what looks bad

We need the time
To draw aside
When turmoil overwhelms
For when we do
We will find peace
In scenic wonder too
I looked out at the view
Across the lake that day
And cast my eye
To just beyond
The mountain's floor
For nestled there
A bright expanse
Most grouped as one
Yet some alone
Stood scattered there
As dots of white
It linked for me a scenic
And most wondrous sight
I gazed, I drew my breath
I drank it in once more
And as I did, I voiced my praise
For Your great splendour Lord

If people ask, how are you friend?
Should I reply at all?
For if I say I'm in great pain
I've got a wound so deep
They're bound to ask
And show their love
But can I simply say
What hurt it was
Inflicted me today
And would they really understand?

Why should I have to suffer this
And she pursue us both?
'What' is the charge
She tries to thrust
To cut and turn
In bitterness
To hurt each one the most?

She calls me hard
Accuses, shrieks
Insists, demands
Makes threats

She jibes and goads
Is bitter, crude

Objecting when we dare to say
We really think your conversation
"Inappropriate this day"
"Oh, there you go, you raise the past

You really need to get a life!"
But she for ten whole minutes long
Complained, bemoaned her lot

I tried to steer the positive
To voice support and prayer
Of 'being there' for her
But still she ranted on and on
Until finally I commented
Behaviour over years
Has reaped this very song
And that was it
Her fury leapt
And rage
It overflowed
While silent tears
As usual
Dropped down inside my heart

IN THE QUIETNESS SPEAK LORD

Lord, thank you for this time with You
For all Your grace, and comfort too
It's only in my drawing near
That I can listen, I can hear

I want You Lord to speak to me
Then I'll become what I should be

So please come now, and touch my heart
And will You, Lord, Your Word impart
Holy Spirit, strengthen me
Fill me now, empower me

THE JUDGMENT OF JEREMIAH

If the warning is heeded
Then judgment's not needed
If the nation repents
Then God says He'll relent
But blessings intended
They never attended
That kingdom, that nation
That was My creation

I could have remoulded
But sadly you folded
My plans to raise you
Did not embrace you
All those wrongs you have done
Yet you still carry on
Now that is a shame
When you are to blame

You aren't intending
Your ways to be mending
I've had it with you
The things that you do
With your eyes off of me
Now disaster you'll see

RAP OF TRUTH

I gotta declare the truth of God's Son
He became a man, He was the Holy One
You ain't talkin' 'bout no insignificant One!
He's the Boss, He's the Lord, we receive Him as King
When we recognise, yeah, and we take it all in
And you know, that He died, to release us from sin
He rose from the dead, quite amazingly!
He's the great I AM, He's the only key
Who can give us hope so that we can 'be'
He saved us from death and the course we was on
When we travelled down the road of destruction
Now we can testify it's our life He's won!

WILFUL TRANSITION

If we are going to walk in faith
We will need to walk in obedience
It's not a touchy, feely existence
That we have with God
We are believers and followers of God's own Son!
He is the Lord Jesus Christ
We are not just 'convinced' that trusting Him
is the way forward
Faith in Jesus has consequences
It demands action
It demands our obedience
And if, having laid down our hopes
Our aspirations, our fears and failures
Our thoughts and temptations
If we have surrendered our successes
Or distresses, our disappointments
And have then heard God speak to us
And have written down the words He spoke
Then we will need to act on them
This is a time of transition and transaction!
We expected God to speak
He has and He will do so again
Now we need to commit to obeying Him
SO whether that is saying I will not walk in fear
I will trust God in everything
I will walk in forgiveness
I will place my future in God's hands
I will commit to holiness
I will release my loved ones to God
I will follow Him wholeheartedly
THIS is the day of change and transformation!!

RECURRENT CYCLONE

We have a recurrent cycle of silence
Of withdrawal
Followed by confrontation
Then 'blast off'
Sometimes there is peace
Also laughter
The times of connection
Can become time consuming
In a working day
Any insistence drains energy
As well as resources
And it spoils
Peace is interrupted
A 'shift' takes place
That is disruptive beyond measure
Then, spillage amidst anger
Or tears, or maybe both
Followed by rejection that threatens
Rearing its ugly head

HEARTFELT PLEA

Oh Lord, I am crying out to You for help!
Only You can bring her deliverance
You are the One who rescued us
And we know that so many times
When we have been desperate
To hear Your voice
You have answered and brought strength

I can't go on forever wondering what will happen 'if'
It has gone on far too long
I need a definite answer
I am exhausted and in pain because of it
Even though I trust You
My heart needs Your personal word
Please don't let her down

Look after her all the days of her life
And show her Your constant love
Don't let her be angry
Give her understanding Lord
Especially of Your care
Thank You for Your word of 'Peace'
Only You can supply this Peace
In the midst of trial
I release her now to You
I will trust You for You are my God
I will pour out praise to You
No matter what happens

COUNTER CULTURE INHERITANCE

In the Beatitudes Jesus declared
A new way of behaviours
Responses to life's situations
That are 'counter culture'
This 'Kingdom living' is helpful
And practical because it works
It is also encouraging
It covers everything
That we might experience
And it feeds us spiritually
It starts and ends with an inheritance clause
For both the 'poor in spirit' and also for those
Who are persecuted because of 'righteousness'
Both have the assurance
That 'theirs is the Kingdom of Heaven'
Whatever level of suffering you are enduring
Whatever depth of spiritual hunger
Or disconnectedness you are experiencing
God has you in mind
His are the resources available to you
Comfort, spiritual solace and fulfilment
Keys to greater and deeper access of God
Grace, mercy, and true identity through Him
As you put on His clothing
And walk in these ways of grace and of mercy
And humility, purity of thought, word and deed
This is how you will come to be known
As good, honest, caring people
Who have both encountered
And have relationship with God
So don't despair

Tell God all about it
And of course
Be ready to hear what He says

I would if I could Lord
But I stand here bruised
Oft times I'm confused
The things I was certain of
No longer have that power
I am wondering in a desert
Having no sense of direction
It's really scary!
That which I could emphatically declare
Doesn't even seem within my grasp
Your Word is truth, of this I'm sure
Would You take me deeper
Than I have ever been before with You God
Reveal much more
From Your Word of truth
And particularly from Yourself please
That's all for now!

What a week this has been
I was drained before it started
Unable to read my Word at length
Couldn't concentrate
Any quiet time was constantly interrupted
I've had to leap up early to help family
Been behind on my jobs
Tired, lacking in motivation
And I've shed more than a few tears
I'm finding it extremely difficult
Allotting time for this or that
When I don't, you know the score
Everything, yes everything goes haywire
I expect others feel like this from time to time
But for me, this needs to diminish
And I must act and do that which is planned
Then perhaps some order can be re-established
So that I can pursue time for my creativity to flow

CALL OF DUTY

You're always on cod
But what about me
And what about God?

Why should I pick up my clothes
When I see that you don't
Why do you leave a mess?
And I'm not allowed
Isn't that dirty?
I think it's 'disgusting!'
I want to get out
Take walks in the park
Talk, skip and jump
Run, and have fun

WHAT SPARKS A FIRE?

The crossing was as calm as a mill pool,
Quite unlike our temperaments
So what sparks a fire?
An explosion in your life
What sparks any fire?
You must be aware I'm sure
That the drier the wood
The easier it is to burn
When you are overly tired
When weariness consumes

This is the time, if not checked
Or immersed in a blanket of prayer
To so easily release a torrent of words
Or emotion that should have stayed within
your frailty!

HEALTH & SAFETY APPAREL

There's a layer of insulation I put on
Between the normal coat that I wear and myself
It's not just because the weather has turned cold
and icy
It's actually for protection
It is due to their ice cold rejection
And their silence
The trouble is that protection of this nature
Isolates me from trust and faithfulness
So I had better take it off again Lord
And dress in what is familiar and recognisable
So that I can feel and experience Your love
For that's where I am secure and safe

The explosion was sudden
and words gushed out in profusion
Like a torrential downpour from stormy skies
Then words of defence turned back
on the so-called 'accuser'
But, was the question an accusation?
Should it have even been spoken
Should it have been rephrased
How should it have been addressed
For if one's curiosity should open
the floodgates even a fraction
What help is there for the individuals
in the wake of that flow?
And should they be consumed
with the surge that ensues?
For what purpose may I ask?
Was this supposed to be a lesson in democracy
to highlight fault?
And why wrap all past conversations
In one single sheet as though to prove a point?
How this contradicts all behaviour with others
Is this supposed to be the better path, the path of love?
Is therefore wisdom denied to one's treasured possession
And course sandpaper used
to erase an 'apparent' accusation?
What gauge of accuracy has been used in this instance?
It is not the laser of the Spirit, that's for sure
Unless in introspection it inwardly reveals
The hatred of failure and words of any sort
That do highlight such a glimmer of light
Upon supposed inadequacy

For what other reason would one attack
Presumed accusation with destructive words
And allow the rage within the light of expression?
There is no need to vent all wrath
When truly absence of criticism runs through the core
Of any love for you my friend

REMORSEFUL ADDICT

It's not helpful
This insistence of mine
I need to stop it now
This launching into defence mode
When I feel I'm being attacked
And that's when anger strikes it's chord
Relentless repeat patterns
Outbursts, silence, anger stored
Sadness apparent
Nothing shared
Until later
To settle account
Restore a level of peace

NO RETRIBUTION

Retribution - ain't no solution
Gotta go God's ways, always
No planning 'n schemin'
No wrong ways or dreamin'
'Cos you know if you do
You'll be seen like them too!
'Troublemakers,' that's all that they is
'Fools' lookin' into others' business
Best not be jealous of those that are bad
'For if you do that, you'll only be sad
That's not what God wants for you, not at all
He loves you so much, now 'Follow!' His call
Put trust in Him, your Heavenly Father
Sing songs of praise, or pray if you'd rather
Keep focused on what you's supposed to be learnin'
Pursue what is good, trust in God, and keep yearnin'
Seek Him, it's the best thing
You know I'm not jestin'
'Gonna say Amen?'
'Well, that's alright then!'

NO BANNERS

Did you think that we should display
Banners to welcome you home
Sing, wave and shout
Upon your return
When your heart
Distanced remained
No apology or explanation made

You think that you can do as you please
And not as you should at your age
You know, time escapes
Like the morning mist
It evaporates hope
It distances trust
From the closeness of family
That you know should exist

Your wilfulness stole so many years
Left in its wake such a gaping sorrow

That no blanket of comfort could ease
Now we stand here
So stripped and bare
Deep in sorrow
But not without care for you

Where is God's love
I plead once again
His Light to restore one's soul
Let it spring forth
We implore you O Lord

With Your hope that endures
To quicken our steps

SOAK IN GOD'S PRESENCE

I don't know why but you came to mind
As you seek the Lord you will truly find
Treasures within His Word to direct
Strength and power to others affect
Soak in God's presence, allow His embrace
May the Lord fill you with more of His grace!

JEWELS IN YOUR CROWN

As I sit here thinking, praying for you
I am strongly aware of how deeply the Father loves you
I can see a crown embedded with some beautiful jewels
To which He is adding more
They shine and they sparkle
It is time I believe
He would say to you
That you should know
You are indeed precious to Him
For you are! So now be assured
For there is nothing that He does not see
Of your love and your care
And, how could you doubt
That salt and light do not robe you!

Even though we do not meet
We do not greet you as before
It does not mean we neither care
Nor think nor pray dear one
For when we hear of your distress
It causes pain
For we remain beyond the shore
Some distance from deep fellowship
That once we knew
And yet, we send to you our love
We pray for healing of your grief
We ask the Lord for some relief
To breathe again
To hear His voice
Receive His touch
Drink deep of Him
And in His very Presence soak
Put on his cloak of righteousness
And dwell within His shelter there

CHARADES

Friend, what you say
Seems nought but empty words
Few are wise, most are strewn in haste
They are as refuse, seated in bin liners
Collected but not delivered
To their proper destination
Just rotting there and yet
You are not devoid of hearing
Intellect or wit
For when applied comes learning
With knowledge, even humour

Seldom does one view these truths
For barriers erected there
Conceal the lonely hidden man
Who tries futile to impress
Forgetting those he leaves behind
In sadness and in sorrow deep
Is it too late to make amends?
It does seem so, unless he turns
And places trust in God Who heals
And seeks direction there
Once more to yield and to obey
If only he would follow on
Lay down complaint and anger strong
Submit and say 'You are the Lord
In Whom I trust, I will obey
And read Your Word
I will forgive, release and choose to learn!'

PURELY INSECURITY

Time to retreat again
Say not one more word
Or false accusations fire
Completely absurd!
It makes me quite sad
It spoils and it wrecks
How can God's gift to you
Make you so vexed?
'Think' when you comment
'The kids can't be told!'
So, how are you different?
Except you are old

JESUS SAID 'FEAR NOT!'

It's only God can calm us
E'en when fears alarm us
Yet in His Presence near
He wipes away each tear
It's not that we don't trust
But draw on Grace we must

TRUST IS NOT EASY

Please, do not worry, have no fear
You surely know that God is near
You may not feel His Presence close
And maybe hope diminished is
But you are God's Own precious one
Yes, you dear friend
And you are His

DAMAGED BUT NOT FORGOTTEN

It's hard to explain such loss with no gain
When few understand that 'innermost' pain
The heartache, dashed hopes, it's incredibly sad
Hard to relinquish, and much harder be glad
Yet God has us each enwrapped and held tight
And He knows, yes He sees, everyone's plight
So we'll continue to pray
For each other, each day

HEAVENLY HUG FOR A VICTIM

I remember still
Those years long past
I wanted, yearned
For your embrace
I didn't know, had no idea
How it could be
That you violated
Yes, you destroyed
What trust I had
And she, who once did love you true
Disgust – in silent thought of you
It was no background now I see
Foundation sure for strong belief
When you, sarcastic turned on God
And yet, salvation it stayed strong
The Father's heart for me and all
That was so very strong and rich
And also true and free
To heal, bring life
And actually allowed me 'Be'

WAYSIDE FLOWER

I am like a flower
Fallen on the wayside
Pick me up Lord
And put me in Your vase
There for all to see
Your beauty shed within
It's not what I've achieved
It's submission to You, Lord
And how I've been transformed
By the power of Your Word
And still, I feed on You
That's all that I can do
Let Living Waters flow
Infusing every cell
With Your Resurrection power
So Your wonders I might tell!

IN THE SILENCE

There are times when silence heavy lies
It does not mean that care or prayer has vanished
Far from it
Contemplation leads us most times
To the Father under whose wings we find shelter
Yes, it is dark there
For we cannot see beyond the shade of His love
All we know is that we are protected in Him
There are no distractions, there appears no guidance
What we do know is how precious we are to Him
We can bring our confusion
Our sadness, the heat of our anger
There is nothing He does not understand
We pray on

GET INTO THE BOAT

So where are you at?
Are you thriving or driving
Surviving or striving?
Stopped for a drink
Oh, let me think
You must remember
To trust in God's Presence!
He's there in the boat
Hasn't left you afloat
He commanded the waves
And He stilled the storm
You know the scriptures
You know the form
It's Peace that you need
It's Peace as you breathe
It's no stress or distress
So don't settle for less!
Yes, the battle it rages
You'll know the attack
But Who's in command here
Why should you lack?
There's more for you friend
'Cos with God there's no end
There's nothing to fear
For you know God is near
So calm yourself down
Now 'put on' Christ's gown!

STILL NEED HEALIN'

I gotta put it down yeah, put it down, yeah, put it down
'Cos this anger ain't doin' me no good, it ain't helpin' me
No ways, I said 'no ways, it's no good!'
Think I'm okay one day
I can shut that door once and for all,
then what do I find?
D'you mind, do you care, didn't ask you to call
An' now I can't stop myself, wanna kick, wanna scream
I gotta say they're ain't no help, no in between
You can't see my hurt, my confusion
But for me it ain't no illusion
Yet, I'm the one gotta be quiet, yeah with no riot
Not speak about it, gotta quit talkin' 'bout it
But it's tough, yeah rough, no rebuff, had enough
Know what I mean? There's no in between
Some day, one day, expect I'll understand
'Til then, you know, I'm gonna need a hand
So will You help me, yeah help me,
'Cos I need Your peace
I want comfort, some space
Yeah for this release
Now help me please God, 'cos I'm beggin' You
It's You I need God, will You help me through.

A FEW WORDS TO ENCOURAGE

Let not sorrow come dear friend
In this hour of need
Be assured you're loved of God
Only on Him feed
Trusting as you're walking onward
Faith is tested, yes, that's true
Walking with the Master, Jesus
Is the journey to pursue

This journey is lengthy Lord
I've travelled and toiled
Sought help from You, Saviour
And what have I found?
Though the path is not easy
And the incline is steep
You're there by my side
Every step that I take
Oft times I've forgotten
How You're faithful and true
Oh! Let me remember
Everything that You do

THE CANVAS OF MY LIFE

If I were to paint my thoughts
What should they be and what should I include
What colour is grief upon my landscape
What hues of happiness, joy and laughter
Might there be clouds of doubt and of perplexity
With those endless plans of intent half complete
Will my finished brush strokes
Like threads on a garment, joined up patterns
Reflect hope or even laughter
Can such a painting redirect one's sadness
Even confusion
Can it redefine love with inclusion's embrace
For that is how You are with me Lord
Let the canvas of my life reflect this same grace

NAIL BITING STUFF

What should one do when loneliness strikes it's chord
'despair'
And no-one calls and hope seems distant still
Who knows the sadness that prevails
The one who suffers loss
These hidden depths though not revealed
By word of mouth, are known by God Who cares
And my heart weeps to see your pain
Your fingernails each bitten deep into the quick
Such blood stained years of grief that you have borne
Yet, still you carry on in life determined
to fulfil your dreams
How brave, such focus strong
But then I sense you are bereft while there alone
Despite the years now spent
You have your memories it's true, your intellect and wit
But can you say you are fulfilled
And what of your dismay
Your heart that cries in silent woe
You may not wish to ask of God who knows you well
He longs that you accept salvation rich
He bought for you at costly price
That carried all your pain
It cost His Son His life, His death
To purchase hope and love and joy
Relationship with you

Accept this sacrifice of love from Him
And choose the path of freedom
Purchased with the Saviour's blood
The Father wants to walk with you, He does
Now, will you walk with Him?

CORRECTING VISION

Specs' for the eyes will improve one's vision
'Specks observations' just cause division
You need a good heart
For you to stay smart
That's the best condition
To receive recognition
To show grace is right for every situation
As behaviour reflects one's faith's presentation
Your witness is proof of your innermost being
And nothing is hidden from those that are seeing
Perhaps if you're true to the fruit you display
They will see God's goodness to us all each day

TAPESTRY

Before I die
Let me explain
I've lived,
I've gained
Through grief
Through pain
These truths are hard
For some to bear
But I the richer
Have become

DIRECTION REQUIRED

As I meet with You this morning
Will you speak to me
Will You point the way to follow
Give direction please
I'm asking You to show me clearly
Precisely what to do
You've directed me so often
Please now see me through
It's hard for me to make decisions
With all that's going on
In my muddled state of mind
Now help me to be strong

WORDS

When you're not sure
What to say
Look no further
I have words
Words of truth
That bring you comfort
Words to express
Your every thought
Words
Whether in grief
And continued lament
You need words
To release these feelings
I can help
Now just relent

A PLACE OF SAFETY

Come away with me a while
To a place of peace
Where you can draw aside
Let go of fears
Of worries, all cares
The baggage you've carried
Throughout the years
Only come to Jesus
Your Saviour, your Lord
Trust simply in Him
In His powerful Word
That's where you'll find comfort
Direction, deep joy
Every aspect of life
There for you to employ

How bad was the damage?
And what was included?
Abuse verbal or physical
Should be excluded
What about morals?
What about truth?
Nothing expressed
No apologies made
Just ranting
And shouting
Seclusion was paved
I was frightened and sad
I had to do this
I had to do that
Silenced and separated
Though I was not bad

NO BLOSSOM, NO FRUIT

I heard someone say 'No Blossom No Fruit'
They seemed really powerful words
It's simply the truth of God and creation
But is it reflective of us?
I think it could be
It certainly might
For I long what I am should reveal
The goodness of God
His beauty, His truth
Producing this fruit in my life

TAKE THE MEDICINE YOURSELF

Everything you do is seen
Everything you are is known
Take the medicine yourself!
The discipline that should be yours
How foolish is the hypocrite
Whose selfishness is seen by all
Except they fail to view themselves
To value 'time' that quick is lost

WHEN HOPE IS LOST

When hope is lost
In disappointment's gain
All quests for healing
Somehow all restrained
Direct and help me
Please Lord, I request
Without Your Joy
I am but visionless

LIKE THE BUTTERFLY

There is a beauty within
Each creation God has made
And we sometimes catch a glimpse
From the colours there displayed
Now, if we will allow God
Our lives to shape and mould
We'll be a lovely vessel
More valuable than gold
And 'that' will be our beauty
The work that GOD has done
Because we have surrendered
Our all to God's own Son

HIDDEN HOPE

Could I, would you allow me
To spend a little time with you
I know that is difficult for you
I am only here for these few days
And you have to remain here
In this place of safety
While I go back home
Any sense of love and warmth you feel is true
Believe me
That is so hard for you to comprehend
When you have been betrayed
By the ones who should have stayed forever
Throughout your childhood days
We push pain away when it hurts so deeply
Who can face such suffering after all?
How can one address it 'in time?'
No, you don't just 'grow up'
And somehow it disappears
You can't grow out of pain

TROUBLES AND TRIALS

When I contemplate the troubles and trials
Sometimes in heartache
Though sometimes in smiles
What we have been through
Over all these years
Yet we're still knotted together
Despite endless tears
Our love has deepened
Our faith it has grown
Yes, we pressed deep into God
From those seeds that were sown
We are knitted together
God planned it this way
You're one valued person
There's nothing can sway
The love that we have
Remains and is true
Dearest love
We're so very proud of you

A GIFT UPON THE ALTAR

Please let my words be precious
As I give them
Not necessarily orally Lord
But those I write in my heart
And in my book for everyone
Each and every individual
That needs to hear and build trust
So they may really know
The riches You supply
Yearning then for more, yes Father
For Your endless supply feeds
Overwhelms when received
As does revelation
Of the way You see us
Encouraging our lives so much
More understanding of Your majesty
Power and might previously unknown
And an outpouring
In response of worship and words
That both edify and encourage endurance
Reveal Your heart for us
Moment by moment
Through every single expression of need
That we have - And as we allow You
Take our heartaches
And our aspirations totally Lord

I've always hated shouting
I remember as a child
Such voices raised
Their voices loud
I cried a silent scream
Please will you stop!
I'm pleading from within
I hate it when you do that
It causes tears to flow
It makes me feel quite angry
It makes me feel so sad
And yet somehow they turn on me
They pour frustrations out
It leaves me so distressed
I'm not sure what to do
For if I speak
Release my grief
They'll surely scream at me
And then I will be locked away
They'll shout
And stomp once more
Their banging of the doors
Is all so very strange
Inside my head
You know O Lord
I can't control my thoughts my pain
I'm hurting all the more
Please help me now Lord Jesus!
I'm emptied to my core

DESPAIR NO MORE

I feel I need to clarify
The feelings that one has
To express in words, emotions
For the reasons we are sad
For when we're spent, discouraged
We're trapped inside ourselves
Those memories we've had locked in
The wretched waste of years
The thoughts of hurt
That we've suppressed
Our sadness, all our fears
Yet there is hope
For each of us
If we will seek we'll find
And joy will come
As well as peace
For each one misaligned
And 'How is that?'
You ask me
My testimony's clear
You only have to trust in God
Who takes away all fear

FOR THE WEARY

Happiness is available
To all those who seek the Lord
Direction can be found
As we dwell upon His Word
Joy can be attained
By our trust in the Saviour
Obedience to all He says
Will enable our behaviour
Ensuring trust increases
Is the way that we travel
Enabling fear to vanish
And our doubts to unravel
So we give to God our fears
And also all our sadness
Coming boldly to the throne
With complete and utter gladness

WRONGLY ACCUSED

So you object
You 'think' I judge
Though I do silent speak
Yet judge you do
Raising your tone
And everyone can hear

So, who is right?
And who is wrong?
Now, please remember this
'Perception' cannot ably voice
The heart of her accused
Or rectify the inner pain
That uninvited comes
That rises up and gushes out
When triggered suddenly

Did she tell him how I ask
She voiced aloud
Her judgment
There of me
Before that crowd?
When I in silence
Viewed that scene
Was distressed
I wanted to scream?

Should I reach out
For you to shout?
And did you know 'you' judged?
What right have you to tell me off?

You disrespect me so
It's not your place to 'deal' with me
Shout or shrieking follow me
When all I do is try my best
But I still human am

A POEM TO ENCOURAGE

I need not be afraid
For Lord You've heard my prayer
And even though I'm anxious
You promise to be here
In every thought
With every step
You speak
You guide me on
So as I venture out this day
I'll seek to follow You
In trust, in faith
I'll walk the path
With You beside me Lord
I will not fear
But look to You
For You will see me through

BITTER SWEET

We've noticed so much tension
In past weeks and months and years
You may think that we don't love you
While you carry many fears
You wear the clothes
You answer 'Yes'
But is that really true?
It's only God Who sees beneath
As only He knows you
And only He can heal your wounds
And those for whom you care
We pray one day you'll know within
That yes, we've all been there
We love you and we always have
We bless you, yes, we do
We pray that you will turn to God
To trust He'll see you through

RENEWAL REQUIRED

I feel I'm in no man's land
The desert is sparse
I've lost all direction
Nothing is planned
Help me please
My focus renew

CHANGE OF CLOTHING

What pain is felt deep
When history repeats
It hastens expulsion
From all the familiar
For love that's now lost
Its security breached
The challenge 'pursuit'
To press deep into trust
Provides us a doorway
For faith to develop
It's time that we knew
That God moulds us
He shapes us
He offers us purpose
A future at last
Our souls to renew
Release from the past

TIME IN HIS PRESENCE

Do not worry, do not fear
You surely know that God is near
He longs for you to be at peace
Now, all your fears to Him release
You do not have to do, to be
He bids you 'Rest!' now, can't you see
Release your hurts to Him this day
And keep forgiving come what may
You're blessed of God and 'special' too
Each day is precious, so are you
Stay in His presence, there 'at rest'
Where there's no tension, that's what's best
No need employing endless tasks
Just 'you with Him' is all He asks
So try, make time, to draw aside
For that's the place you will abide

PERMISSION NEEDS COMMISSION

Permission needs commission
From the presence of the Father
For equipping by the Spirit
For empowering if you'd rather
For we cannot
And we should not
Plan of our volition
But repent
And seek the Lord
In an act of pure contrition

CREATIVITY'S FLUTE

Is it audacious to think it ungracious
To eliminate creativity in my life?
To think that I may greater succeed
With critique assessments
For others to feed
In my opinion this isn't success
It purely employs
The writer's distress
It damages one
From proceeding to gain
Heartfelt response
From sadness and pain
Expressed in poetic words to reveal
Truth that would otherwise be concealed
So I've not pursued academia's route
Traversing instead Creativity's flute
Its sounds resonating in one's heart
All kinds of emotion to others impart

SPECTACULAR BLOSSOM

The blossom
It just reminds me of you
So thankful to God
In all that you do
The colour, the splendour
God's gift of abundance
Surely radiates joy
And the light of His presence
Transcendent in beauty
It falls silent down
A wonderful carpet
Of love all around!

REWARDS OF CHANGE

When you have to live
A completely different way
Whatever the reason
Or even the dismay
You are definitely not abandoned
And certainly not by God
You can feed upon His Word each day
Following in the steps Christ trod
And if you seek His presence
He will daily strengthen you
He'll comfort in the grief
Sustain you in the trial
You need to be reminded
To rest in Him a while

STIFF NECKED CHARADE

What powerless ammunition
You endless aim and fire
When all your long term issues
Unresolved are
For all these years
You've not moved on
You say you have
In happy song
Yet ignorance and disrespect
Beneath disguise of sheer neglect
Come on now, wake up, live, repent
For wasted years without relent
Of so called 'issues' hidden fast
It's time for each to now be cast
For God brings freedom
True release
And Jesus came
To bring true Peace

ANGRY

Childhood memories murky rise
I splutter, I mutter and angry I shout
Horrid reactions
Banging, retorting
Doors still on hinges
Revenge for the past
For what provocation
I hate accusation
For long I've been silent
But damage that lingers
Has surfaced again
This time is for cleansing
For healing, for wholeness
I pour out my pain
And now give it to God
Oh Lord, would You touch me
Completely renew me
Mend all that is broken
And heal me this day

LET ME WALK THE PATH

Let me walk the Saviour's path
All the days of my life
Whatever may befall
Be it peace or even strife
For we are none of us exempt
Of the woes that come along
Yet we can fix our minds
To rejoice in happy song

A SPIRITUAL TRANSACTION

It's a spiritual transaction
Asking Jesus in
Accepting Christ as Saviour
To be Lord and King

Life can never be the same
When God has entered your heart
Your vision is changed
God's Word becomes clear
Refreshment is only the start

NO PLACE FOR JUDGMENT

It's not our place to judgment proclaim
We need to know that is God's domain
What's needed from us
Is to release from the past
Forgiveness and grace
Is the truth that will last
Especially for those
Who have made wrong decisions
They've yet to advance
And mature in reactions
To parent their child
With responsible actions
And what about us
What do we have to do?
Support and encourage them
Their journey through!

WEIGHT BEARING

What burdens should we carry
When the task is heavy Lord?
We're so glad You walk beside us
For You share the load, You do
In fact, it's You Who bears the weight
We can't carry it ourselves
So help us please to keep in step
While 'yoked' this journey through

MERRY GO ROUND

Is it any wonder that we are confused?
I'm not saying that we are never bemused
But so often we just sit and stare
Out at that plateau of total despair
Pondering thoughts, pondering life
While deep inside we are suffering strife
Yet when mercy begins to strike its chord
In gratitude we can begin to applaud
As our hearts are changed
To joy and not sadness
For that's when people
Can then view our gladness

TREE ROOTS FOR GROWTH

You must know
That what's been sown
Has now grown
Its roots gone deep
The tree displays
For all to see
Maturity
It upward grows
With branches wide
A wondrous sight
Displaying strength
Beneath is shade
Through every season
Even strife

UNCERTAIN CERTAINTY

Grasping at straws guarantees nothing
Nothing but heartfelt distress
What happened there at oncology please
When she went there that day for review
'The cancers aggressive' ... was his response
She wept in dismay at such news

Destructive in force
Of darkened decline
That of a hammer blow
Her thoughts like a maze
Could eliminate hope
But strangely that wasn't the case

For she herself is content and at peace
As she ponders the future, her life
The effect on her family, also her friends
The cause and effect of such strife
It raises the question for each one of us
To consider how life it will end

ASSISTANCE REQUIRED

Lord please will You come to my aid
I'm struggling
I don't know why
All that I know
Is I'm feeling so sad
My strength it saps and runs dry
I seem to have lost all hope in my life
Will You please lift up my chin
Direct me, correct me
Release all my grief
And gladden the eyes of my heart
I know that You alone can deliver
With the strength I've found in Your love
So I'm asking You once again O God please
Feed me and I shall be fed!

STAIN REMOVAL

My hopelessness surrounds me still
Take away my grief and my hurt
All this pain
My anger
My sense of loss
That continues time and again
I know I too am guilty
For I've not let them go
Those accusers that I must release
Enable me now to employ Your grace
Or I will never know peace
And I will be bound by their actions of hate
That would entrap with nothing to gain
I need transformation as I want to live
Now please rub away this stain

A PLEA FROM THE HEART

What do you know of my innermost ponderings
Are you acquainted with my mental wanderings
How came you thus to your set ideas
Have you also restled with these my fears
Some of the pains I know we have shared
Through deepest griefs you sincerely have cared
You have heard me and held me
Your comfort I've found
Even when I have hardly uttered a sound
But now, storm tossed seas seldom come near our shore
Any yet, there's a battle rages inward, what's more
It doesn't die down but becomes more intense
It can't be contained, it makes little sense
Except that we learn together again
Is that so hard, does that cause you pain
Don't you want to discover just what I've become
I'm more than a housewife and more than a mum
Yes, I need to express what I feel here inside
To converse with you, laugh and also confide
To discover truth, seek the way ahead
Not fearing the future, but being lead
Trusting God together in our times of need
That's all I'm requesting and for this I plead

LORD CHANGE ME

Help me to be free to live
And make me more able to forgive
Help me to walk the way of love
Empowered with grace that comes from above
Break those chains that bind me Lord
Break my old nature with Your sword
Cut out that sinful stubborn will
That nurses hurt and makes me ill
I repent now Lord
I choose a different way
I want to follow You
In all that You say
For only then will I become whole
In pursuit of You my one true goal

WHAT TALENT

What happens when you hide your talent?
In a hole in the ground
Where nothing of the gift you've been given
Is in there to be found

Is it too late to renovate
That skill again I ask
How many years has it taken?
To now commence this task

PLEASE TO ADVISE

When you're down
And you are weary
Sleep deprived
And often teary
It's not helpful to debate
You're not able in 'a state'
To come off all medication
That won't be pure jubilation!
Ask the Lord please to advise
Timing's key now, no surprise!
He will show you what to do
When and how, to see you through
Through to Glory
What a story!

WASTED YEARS

Oh, the wasted years
When we hide away
All our tears
Doing nothing at all
Too resolve
Our resentment
Including those of our fears

I'm not saying
We should fuel the fire
Or stir revenge
Entrap the liar
No, it's really
Far more basic friend
Forgiveness based
It's time erased

SET YOUR MIND

Try to delve a little deeper
Into God's Word
If you set your mind
To do so
Your heart
It will be stirred

You need to make the time
Dear friend
It's important
Don't you see
You need to look to Jesus
To completely set you free

RAGING STORM

It's been a stormy few days
In so many ways
The weather will sometimes reflect
The rages within
The doubts
The frustrations
The unresolved issues we have
I believe this is true
I need help, so do you
But how do we deal
With this trial I ask
Do we turn to the Spirit for help
Will we seek guidance
For depth, understanding
In order for change I ask
History has shown
That our speech
And our actions
In order to bear any weight
Need wisdom from God
To influence others
Transform us from this state

HARVEST GROWTH

Reconciliation dispels retaliation
For a harvest to grow
You must first sow the seed
Feed it with truth
And with prayer
Water it too
Speak words of life
Not complaint
For if you do that
It will not bring forth gain
Except God's displeasure, delay
Disobedience
Will never comply
With growth and belief
So don't wonder why
Just trust in what's sown
That you have since owned
For a harvest of blessing for all

MIND TRICKS

The effective corrective
In cases of pain
Is to find the root cause
For health once again
For, if you know that
And how to repair
You soon will improve
To rise up from there

SMART REASSURANCE

Just think of yourself
As a shining light
Yes, a light that shines
That is brilliant and bright
When the sun goes in
And you are sad
Turn on your light
Dismiss what is bad
Those things people say
Just aren't true
You should know
You are actually clever
From head to toe
So stand up
Look people straight in the eye
The ones that hurt you
Will stop with a sigh
We know you're intelligent
We know you're smart
Just look how you build
And look at your art

Your Word
Like pure spring water
Refreshes my soul
And strengthens me
You give wisdom
Also insight
Direction each day
As I read
As I seek
I confess
Though You know
Without Your instruction
I would be weak

VALUED CHILD

We don't know if you realise
Perhaps it comes as no surprise
To know how much
We care for you
You're valued
You should know that's true
We want you
To succeed in life
With peace and healing
Without strife
So on this day
We wish you well
We pray that God
In you will dwell
For that's the way
You'll know real peace
And joy will flow
That will not cease

NIGHTMARE

I had a dream
And in that dream
I was there
In that place
It was almost like
An unreal world
Having to be totally silent
Where I was not to be heard
Not even to be seen by him
It was all so very absurd

It was not an experience
I would want to repeat
As I couldn't be me
Nor that child to greet

It was as if all had to be done
To a plan, a set plan
And it just wasn't normal
It was not, no one can

Also, there was fear in place
Couldn't step out of line
Had to move forward
When nothing was fine
Then when I awoke
It felt bad ... it was dark
I felt ever so sad
That's not the way
Of a family time
To step out of line

Like committing a crime

You've got to be free
To throw off restraint
Or it's not gonna work
No ain't, no, it ain't

LIFE IS WORTH LIVING

When you think that life is no more
You must not listen
When you believe
That you have no worth
You must reject that thought
You are of value
Significant too
We count you as special
We see how you've grown
You have such skill you should know
Would you remember that please
Now will you look to the future
Turn your back on the past
It's time to start living once more
Rise up from that grave
You're no longer beguiled
For you are one precious child

GROWTH FACTOR

Growth comes
At times we can't measure
Unheeded, stalled
It won't produce treasure
To succeed in life
You have to move forward
To see the potential
To expand and develop
These are the tactics
One needs to employ
Especially management
For future and joy
All inclusive development
Expansion, increase
Such active involvement
Can each one release

HUNGER STRIKES ITS CHORD

Lord, I'm hungry and seeking
So often weak
I'm weepy
And I'm struggling
I've found it difficult
To worship at all
But I have done so
Despite this dark cloud

So many times
I find myself praying
Lift this heaviness
From me I plead
Give me some clarity
To help with my thinking
I need some sanity
You know that God

Forget all my tears
They come and go
I just ask Your assistance
To go forward from here

A MOTHER'S PLEA

I take note as always
I'm watching her sadness
Her frustration and anger
Pent up distress and her grief
Would You please Help Lord
Take all these things from her
Help her know mercy, happiness, peace
If she could only
Be released from revenge
Then she could be rescued I'm sure
I have to keep asking
Lord will You help her
Personally save
From this downhill decline

DOWNHILL DECLINE

I think it is one of the hardest things
That we have endured in our lives
Watching there that innermost grief
In your child as part of her life
Though things had been building
Or so we had thought
The atmosphere, it became tense
We witnessed so sadly
Our daughter withdrawing
Her rejection and hateful remarks
This made her feel worse
She had frightening dreams
That we, even might die
Isolated, sad, she really believed
That she would be blamed for our death
She could not just grasp that she could be loved
And continued in her distress
When she wrote that note of apology Lord
We wept and continued in prayer
We longed when she left that she would know
That our love and Yours still remained
We asked that You would accompany her
Because Lord, You've always been there

We don't know if they realise
It surely should be no surprise
That though there's been so many trials
We walked with them for miles and miles
Throughout it all we've had to trust
In God alone
That's been a must
And you can too
In everything
The Lord Almighty is His name
He took our sin
He took our blame
So, turn to Him in your despair
Your hope once more
He will repair

WEARY TRAVELLERS

Drink in the love of Jesus
Drink in the love of God
For He comes with might to bless you
With the power of His Blood

His Grace is available
His might and His power
For this seed that's within you
Can be accessed hour by hour

So take heart
All weary travellers
Jesus came to rescue you
To strengthen
Bring deliverance
Expressed in love for you

Come away with me a while
To a place of peace
Where you can draw aside
Let go of fears
Of worries and cares
The baggage you've carried
Throughout the years
Only come to Jesus
Your Saviour, your Lord
Trust simply in Him
In his powerful Word
For that's the place
Where you will find comfort
Direction, His peace
And deep joy

NEVER WILL I LEAVE YOU

I used to be so frightened
But Jesus talks to me
I'm not sure where I'm going
But Jesus walks with me
He's never going to let me down
He's there by my side
He knows each of my frustrations
And all the tears I've cried
Yet still He says
He'll never leave
His love is real, it's true
Now that's the love He freely gives
And I can have it too
Lord Jesus, will You heal me
And let me trust again
To enjoy each day You give me
Please take away my pain

ALL SUFFICIENT

It may feel like a tunnel
Treading in the darkness
Isolated, stricken
With a note of hopeless despair
Your life it spans before you
I know you can barely see
You think your efforts hopeless
I tell you they are not
You need to banish
All those thoughts
They are not for you my friend
Does His robe adorn you
With His righteousness
You are certainly not forgotten
Quite the opposite
Are you marked as one obedient
A servant of God
A shining light
Who is greatly loved

EXCEPTIONAL COUPLE

What an exceptional pair
Who've fought many trials
And still with God's grace
You continued for miles
You're both patient and kind
You are faithful and true
Prayerful, considerate
In all that you do
Humility, care
With servant hearts
You pray and you share
What God imparts

EFFECTIVE WITNESSES

Were you inspired
Fired of God
Gone from strength to strength
Both in prayer
In the Lord
Through this time and its length
What you are
Have become
In your walk with the Saviour
Can be seen
Is effective
By such behaviour
This whole task
You must ask
To continue God's instruction
When He speaks
You can move
Plus, you can function
We are sure this you know
But it's good just to mention!

WORSHIP

For every month
Of every year
We wish you joy
And God's good cheer

For every day
And every night
Know you are special
In God's sight
So as you come
To worship now
You know in reverence
You must bow

Before the king
The King of Kings
Declaring praise
As your heart sings

SHOCK WAVES

I've always hated shouting
I remember as a child
The voices raised
The voices loud
I cried a silent scream

Please will you stop
I ask them
I'm weeping from within
I hate the way you do that
It causes so much pain

It makes me so angry
It makes me feel so sad
And then you guessed
They turn on me
Frustrations they pour out

And I am left distressed
I'm not sure what to do
For if I speak
They shout at me
It causes greater stress

They scream, they shout
They bang all doors
I feel so very strange
I can't control my thoughts
My pain
I'm hurting all the more
So will You help me please

Lord Jesus
I cry out again

MARY BORE JESUS

They say the woman Mary
That she bore God's own Son
Jesus Whom He sent to earth
Salvation to be won

The reason that He came
Was to bring our restoration
From sin's dark divide
Jesus provides
Our complete reconciliation

Relationship once more
Communion with the Father
Confession of sin
Asking Jesus in
Acknowledging God as Creator
Nothing to fear we're God's family now
And certainly not just spectators

YOUR SHELTER IS MY COMFORT

You are worthy to be praised Lord
But I need to praise you more
Though You know my fears
My longings
I'll express each one in words

You take every grief I've ever known
You know my heart, my plea
You give shelter
Comfort too
You empower me

When I need discernment
I know that I should ask
If I don't I'll stay confused
Completely in a mess

You alone enable me
You accompany me aswell
One day I'll witness to this Lord
And such testimony I'll tell

EASTER

We're celebrating Easter
And Christ's Resurrection true
God sent His Son to save us
He died for me and you
The story doesn't end there
He rose up from the dead
Now all the world can know Him
Search the scriptures and be fed
Just ask the Holy Spirit
To reveal God's Word in power
Join with us now rejoicing
At this time and for this hour

COVID RESTRAINTS

It isn't very often
I don't send a reply
Don't think that you're forgotten
She said with a sigh

I hope you're getting better
Each and every day
And that no-one else in that house
Will fall to Covid's prey

BEFORE I DIE LET ME EXPLAIN

When you look at a person with cancer
Pray, what do you see?
Do you see Life or do you see death
And, can I ask
Have you closed the windows of hope
Have you shut the door of faith
And how did you arrive at this conclusion
Was it speculative
Or was it an immediate reaction
Was it borne out of sorrow
And hopeless despair
For the journey of grief
Has been endlessly long

But my friend, let me ask you this
Have you no more room for God?
Have you forgotten His love?
Let me tell you something now
He has not, and could not forget you
I could not have travelled this journey
This long hard road without Him
And it isn't quite over yet
Neither the trauma nor the grief
My only certainty through all the pain
Is my relationship with God and hearing Him speak
That persistent Word, that close embrace
I can truly say with total confidence
This is what I have valued the most

Table of Contents

213